THE GULF
OIL SPILL

by Linda Crotta Brennan

DISCOVERER
ENTERPRISE

Content Consultant
Thomas Azwell
Environmental Scientist
University of California, Berkeley

CORE
LIBRARY

Published by ABDO Publishing Company, PO Box 398166, Minneapolis, MN 55439. Copyright © 2014 by Abdo Consulting Group, Inc. International copyrights reserved in all countries. No part of this book may be reproduced in any form without written permission from the publisher. The Core Library™ is a trademark and logo of ABDO Publishing Company.

Printed in the United States of America,
North Mankato, Minnesota
052013
092013
THIS BOOK CONTAINS AT LEAST 10% RECYCLED MATERIALS.

Editor: Jenna Gleisner
Series Designer: Becky Daum

Library of Congress Control Number: 2013932003

Cataloging-in-Publication Data
Brennan, Linda Crotta.
 The Gulf oil spill / Linda Crotta Brennan.
    p. cm. -- (History's greatest disasters)
ISBN 978-1-61783-957-3 (lib. bdg.)
ISBN 978-1-62403-022-2 (pbk.)
Includes bibliographical references and index.
1. BP Deepwater Horizon Explosion and Oil Spill, 2010--Juvenile literature.
2. Oil pollution of the sea--Mexico, Gulf of--Juvenile literature. 3. Oil spills--
Mexico, Gulf of--Juvenile literature. I. Title.
363.738--dc23
                                            2013932003

Photo Credits: Chris Graythen/Getty Images, cover, 1; US Coast Guard/
AP Images, 4; Gerald Herbert/AP Images, 8; Red Line Editorial, 11, 32;
Patrick Semansky/AP Images, 13; Justin Stumberg/AP Images, 16; Patrick
Semansky/AP Images, 19; Matt Stamey, The Houma Courier/AP Images,
21; Eric Gay/AP Images, 22, 45; Sun Herald, Drew Tarter/AP Images, 25;
Charlie Riedel/AP Images, 26; Dave Martin/AP Images, 29; Charlie Riedel/
AP Images, 31; NASA/AP Images, 34; Press Association/AP Images, 37;
Brian Skoloff/AP Images, 40

CONTENTS

CHAPTER ONE

DRILLING OIL IN THE GULF

On April 20, 2010, BP, a large oil and gas company, was preparing to disconnect the Deepwater Horizon oil rig from the Macondo oil well in the Gulf of Mexico. Suddenly drilling mud spewed across the rig floor. Gas rocketed up the pipes, and the rig began to shake. Two days later on April 22, 2010, the Deepwater Horizon oil rig exploded and sank. But the

The explosion of the Deepwater Horizon oil rig was the beginning of a major disaster in the Gulf of Mexico.

disaster was just beginning. Millions of barrels of oil were leaking into the Gulf of Mexico.

BP and the Macondo Oil Well

BP's Macondo oil well was located directly south of the mouth of the Mississippi River, 48 miles (77 km) off the Louisiana coast. The water at Macondo was almost one mile (1.6 km) deep. Oil-rich sands lay approximately three miles (4.8 km) below the seafloor.

BP knew drilling such a deep well would be challenging. Miles of water and rock pushed down on the oil. This created a tremendous buildup in pressure. Drillers had to carefully counter that pressure or oil and gas could shoot up the well, causing a blowout.

What Is Oil?

Oil comes from tiny plants and animals called plankton that died millions of years ago. They sank to the bottom of the seas and were buried under sand and mud. Over time more and more layers covered them. Pressure from the layers and heat eventually changed the plankton into oil.

BP's History

BP was a huge company. At the time of the spill, it was the fourth-largest company of any kind in the world. It had more wells in the Gulf of Mexico than any other oil company. But there had been a number of accidents at BP facilities. In 2005, 15 men died in an explosion at a BP oil refinery in Texas City, Texas, because of missing safety flares. A year later, a rusted pipeline burst at a BP oil field in Prudhoe, Alaska, creating a major oil spill.

Gulf Open for Drilling

In 2008 President George W. Bush opened up new areas for drilling in the Gulf of Mexico. Today the United States uses approximately 19 million barrels of oil per day, which is more than any other nation in the world. The United States currently produces approximately 5.7 million barrels of oil per day and imports the rest to meet the demand.

CHAPTER TWO

THE NIGHTMARE WELL

BP began drilling the Macondo well in October 2009. The company had started digging with a rig called the Marianas. But on November 9, 2009, Hurricane Ida struck and damaged the Marianas. BP brought in the newer, more modern Deepwater Horizon oil rig on January 31, 2010, to finish the job.

The Deepwater Horizon oil rig replaced the Marianas rig in January 2010. Just three months later, it exploded and sank.

Deepwater Horizon

The Deepwater Horizon was an exploratory rig. Like a huge ship, it was sailed to places scientists thought might have oil. Then the rig would dig a well to find the oil. Once the oil was found, the well was capped. The Deepwater Horizon oil rig would then sail off to its next job and a production rig would come in to extract the oil.

One BP engineer called the Macondo the "nightmare well." The work was six weeks behind schedule and $58 million over budget. But by April 2010, the well was almost finished. The drillers just had to put in the final section of pipe and seal the well. Then the Deepwater Horizon would be disconnected from the well.

Drilling Deep

Drilling a well as deep as the Macondo is risky. A well is like a long steel pipe stuck into a hole filled with pressurized oil and gas. If drillers are not careful, gas and oil can shoot up the pipe and explode.

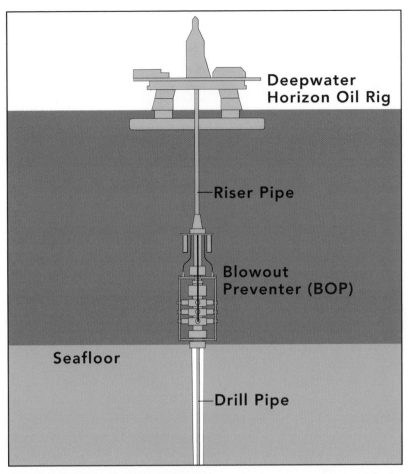

Deepwater Horizon Oil Rig

This diagram shows the Deepwater Horizon oil rig connected to the Macondo well. Locate the BOP. After reading about the blowout, can you picture where the gas and oil shot up from the well?

To prevent a blowout, drillers cement the pipes in place. The cement fills in the space between the pipe and the sides of the well. The cement also plugs the bottom. If there are crevices in the cement job, oil and gas force their way into the well. Each cement job is to be tested. But the cementing job for Macondo's final pipe was never tested for crevices.

Pressure Builds

Before BP disconnected the Deepwater Horizon oil rig on April 20, 2010, they pumped out the drilling mud and replaced it with lighter seawater. Drilling mud is a heavy fluid used to fill the pipes. It is meant to keep pressurized gas and oil from shooting up the pipes.

As seawater replaced the drilling mud, pressure began building in the pipes. Before anyone noticed, drilling mud was spewing all over the Deepwater Horizon's floor. The rig began to shake as gas shot up the pipes. There was a loud hissing noise.

The blowout preventer (BOP) was supposed to close the well and stop gas and oil from coming up the pipeline to the rig. But the gush of gas was already too strong. The BOP failed. The gas was highly flammable. All it needed was a spark from the electrical equipment in the control room to catch fire.

Before the blowout, the BOP was one mile (1.6 km) below the water's surface, near the ocean floor.

Victims

Nine crewmen were on the drilling floor trying to protect their coworkers after the first explosions. They were attempting to shut down the flow of gas through the pipeline. But they were too late. The gas exploded, and they were killed. Two other workers also died. Sixteen more men were severely injured. The bodies of the men killed in the Deepwater Horizon were never found.

Blowout

"Fire! Fire! Fire!" the loudspeaker blared. "Report to emergency stations and lifeboats. This is not a drill." The injured cried for help. Men dove off the platform to escape the flames. Most of the crew of 126 managed to make it to the lifeboats. The rig's supply ship and a nearby fishing boat picked up the ones who had jumped into the sea. But 11 men never made it out.

As tragic as the accident was, it was only the beginning of a major disaster. Where the rig was once connected to the well, a broken pipe stuck out of the seafloor. The pipe was gushing oil into the Gulf of Mexico.

Crane operator Micah Sandell was one of the workers on the Deepwater Horizon oil rig. He explained to investigators what he experienced on the day of the blowout:

> I seen mud shooting. . . . Then it just quit. . . . I took a deep breath thinking that "Oh, they got it under control." Then all the sudden the . . . mud started coming out . . . so strong and so loud . . . it's like taking an air hose and sticking it in your ear. Then something exploded that started the first fire. . . . [The Explosion] . . . knocked me to the back of the cab. I fell to the floor . . . put my hands over my head and I just said, "No, God, no." Because I thought that was it.

Source: Graham, Bob, et al. Deep Water: The Gulf Oil Disaster and the Future of Offshore Drilling, Report to the President. National Commission on the BP Deepwater Horizon Oil Spill and Offshore Drilling. January 2011. Print. 9.

Consider Your Audience

Review this passage closely. Consider how you would adapt it for a different audience, such as your parents, your principal, or younger friends. Write a blog post conveying this same information for the new audience. How does your new approach differ from the original text and why?

CHAPTER THREE

ATTEMPTS TO STOP THE SPILL

The US Coast Guard thought the oil well had been shut down. But as an oily sheen spread across the water, they realized oil was leaking out. BP sent a remotely operated vehicle (ROV) down to the well. The ROV sent back alarming video footage. Oil was gushing from two different places in the broken pipeline. This was a major oil spill.

In some areas, controlled fires were started to burn the oil and help stop it from spreading.

Containment Dome

On April 25, 2010, BP sent robots down to try to activate the BOP. The robots failed. BP tried lowering a containment dome over the leak to trap and collect the oil on May 7, 2010. The oil would be sent up a pipe and collected by tanker ships on the water's surface. But the frigid ocean depths froze and clogged the pipeline.

National Response

Louisiana Governor Bobby Jindal declared a state of emergency. President Barack Obama pledged that the country would use every resource available to contain the oil. The US Coast Guard and US Army were mobilized. Volunteers rushed to the Gulf. More than 45,000 workers helped clean up the Gulf.

Mightier than the Mississippi

After almost four weeks, BP managed to insert a pipe into the well and draw off some of the oil. But the amount of oil the pipe collected made little difference compared to the amount of oil leaking out. This was a much bigger spill than

Large areas of the Gulf were sprayed with dispersants, but the dispersants only removed oil from the surface of the water.

anyone thought, and the oil was heading for shore. The US Coast Guard sent out boats to skim oil from the water's surface. They could only scoop up a small fraction of the oil.

The state of Louisiana opened the Mississippi River's floodgates. This sent a rush of freshwater down the Mississippi River and out into the Gulf. This helped keep the oil offshore. But the oil continued to move toward shore as it gushed unchecked from the well.

Dispersants

BP hired planes to spray the Gulf with dispersants. These chemicals only broke up the oil into small droplets. Instead of floating on the surface, the oil entered the water column. This created problems for animals at sea. And scientists worried that the dispersants might be toxic.

How Much Oil?

In order to respond to the spill, people needed to know how much oil was leaking. BP originally said it was 1,000 barrels per day. Then government scientists said it had to be at least 5,000 barrels per day. In the end, scientists estimated that it was 53,000 to 62,000 barrels per day.

Containment Booms

Boats spread containment booms to keep the oil offshore. Containment booms are plastic-coated fabric tubes made to temporarily hold back floating oil. In calm water, booms work well. But they didn't work well in the Gulf's choppy waters.

BP hired boats to corral and absorb the oil with booms.

Still the booms were visible. They reassured
people that something was being done to help. BP
also had to hire people to lay those booms. Since the
spill had affected the oil industry, the fishing industry,
and tourism, people in the Gulf region were hungry
for work.

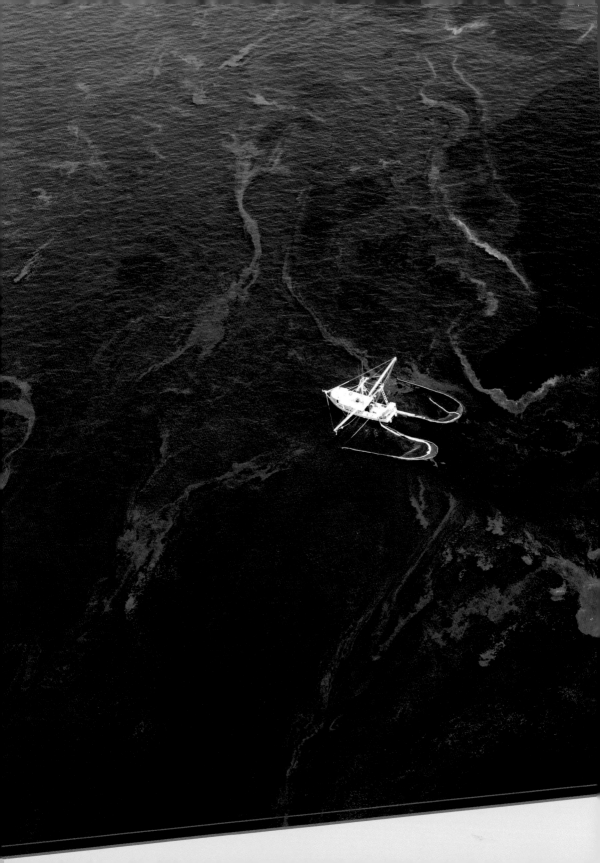

CHAPTER FOUR

OUT OF WORK

The people of the Gulf were still recovering from Hurricane Katrina, which hit in 2005. Now they had been hit by another disaster. Docks that were once busy were now quiet. Many people in the region were fishers. One third of the US oyster and shrimp crop came from the Louisiana coast. The oil spill closed down most of the oyster and shrimping areas.

BP hired fishers to collect oil or lay boom. Instead of fishing for shrimp, this shrimp boat collects oil with booms.

Tourist Industry Suffers

The once bustling streets of the coast were far less busy. A number of people in the Gulf area worked in the tourist industry. But many no longer wanted to vacation on a beach that was covered with oil and tar. Reservations dropped even at hotels in areas with clean beaches.

Unable to Fish

Deep-sea fishers were hurting, too. Almost a fifth of the Gulf was closed to fishing. Even when the fishers could catch fish, few people wanted to buy it. Despite testing and promises that it was safe, people were afraid the fish was fouled by oil.

Oil Workers Out of Work

After the spill, President Obama put a six-month halt to any new drilling below 500 feet (152 m) in the Gulf of Mexico and the Pacific Ocean. He wanted safety measures in place before drilling started again. The oil industry was a major employer. Now even more people were out of work.

Approximately 300 workers, hired by BP, help clean up oil on a beach in Mississippi.

FURTHER EVIDENCE

There is quite a bit of information in Chapter Four about how people were affected economically by the oil spill. What is the main point of the chapter? What are some pieces of evidence in the chapter that support this main point? Visit the Web site below. Does the information on the Web site support the main point of this chapter? Write a few sentences using new information from the Web site as evidence to support the main point in this chapter.

Fishing Industry

www.mycorelibrary.com/gulf-oil-spill

CHAPTER FIVE

EFFECTS ON WILDLIFE

Wildlife on the coast also suffered. The coastlands of Louisiana and the other Gulf states support an incredible variety of plants and animals. The mangrove forests and saltwater marshes serve as fish nurseries. The wetlands are home to pelicans, herons, and egrets. Five different species of sea turtles lay their eggs on the beaches.

Seabirds and other coastal wildlife became trapped in oil.

The oil spill could not have come at a worse time of the year. Spring is the time fish spawn, birds nest, turtles lay eggs, and mammals give birth to their young. Dolphins and sharks started showing up in shallow waters. They were trying to outswim the spreading oil at sea. Hundreds of dead sea turtles began washing up on the beaches.

Gulf States

Although Louisiana was affected the most, eventually oil from the Macondo spill reached all five Gulf states: Florida, Alabama, Mississippi, Louisiana, and Texas. More than 650 miles (1,046 km) of salt marshes, mudflats, mangroves, and sand beaches were oiled.

Sea Turtle Rescue

Mother sea turtles had laid their eggs on Louisiana beaches. Soon those baby turtles would hatch and swim out to oil-filled waters. Volunteers dug up more than 700 turtle nests. The eggs were sent to Florida,

Volunteers placed turtle eggs in coolers lined with sand to relocate them to Florida.

where the baby turtles could hatch and swim out to the clean Atlantic Ocean.

Oil Comes Ashore

On May 19, 2010, oil began washing up along the Gulf shore. Oil slipped around sandbars and came ashore. Crabs suffocated and died in their burrows. During the day, birds soaked in oil roasted in the hot Louisiana sun. Their feathers were no longer able to insulate them, and they died of cold at night. Workers brought the birds to emergency stations where their feathers could be cleaned.

Birdbaths

Saving birds from the oil spill was a long process. Workers had to perform several different steps before releasing them back into the wild, including first collecting the bird and giving the bird a physical exam. Then workers had to warm the bird and give it rest, food, and water. They washed the bird and kept it in an outdoor pool until it fully recovered.

Many birds, such as this brown pelican, were rescued from the oil and cleaned.

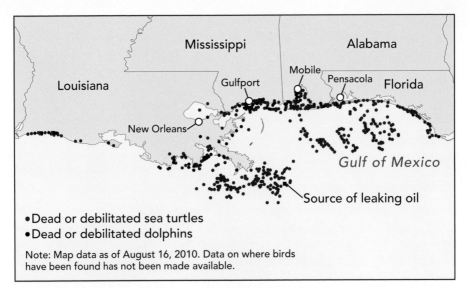

Dolphins and Sea Turtles Affected by Oil

Take a look at this map. When you were reading this chapter, did you imagine the oil spill was this big? Which animals do you think were affected more, the ones out in the Gulf or the ones that lived on the coast?

Lastly, they gave the bird another physical exam before releasing it back into the wild to make sure it could survive.

Photojournalist Gerald Herbert took pictures of the Gulf oil spill. In this excerpt, he describes what he saw at a pelican rookery just after the spill:

> *Pelicans had just come off the endangered species list not too long ago. . . . And it was quite a horror show. Birds were swimming in oiled water. Oil was on the eggs in the nests. Oil was completely surrounding the island and lapping up onto the marsh grass that buffered the mangroves from the sea. And the mangroves are where the pelicans nest.*

Source: "AP Photojournalist Documents 'Horror Show,' Aftermath of Gulf Coast Oil Spill." PBS NewsHour. April 21, 2011. MacNeil/Lehrer Productions, 2013. Web. Accessed December 3, 2012.

What's the Big Idea?

What is Gerald Herbert saying about the effects of the spill on wildlife? Write down two or three pieces of evidence the author uses to make his point. Then write a paragraph describing the point the author is making.

LAST EFFORTS AND LEGACY

Meanwhile, oil still gushed from the pipe at the bottom of the sea. On May 26, 2010, BP tried to top kill the spill by pumping heavy drilling mud into the leak. They also tried to block the well with rubber tire pieces and golf balls. This was called the junk shot. But the flow of oil was too strong. Neither method worked.

This satellite image, taken by NASA on May 24, 2010, shows sunlight reflecting off of the oil spilled in the Gulf of Mexico.

Last Effort

BP engineers and a team of scientists came up with another method to contain the spill. They sent robots down on July 12, 2010, to saw off the top of the broken pipe and place a capping stack over it. The capping stack was similar to a BOP. It would shut off the flow of oil and gas. The engineers had to be careful. When they stopped oil from coming out of the pipe, pressure might build up inside the well. This could cause an underground blowout.

Capping the Spill

The engineers closed the capping stack and watched the pressure carefully. It held steady. So BP decided to inject drilling mud into the well. Then they injected cement to permanently seal the well.

On July 15, 2010, 87 days after it blew, the Macondo was dead. No more oil leaked from the well. But the effects from the blowout would be felt for years to come. An estimated total of 4.9 million

The capping stack, BP's final attempt to stop the oil spill, successfully capped the leaking pipe.

barrels, or 210 million gallons (795 million L), of oil was released from the well.

Broken Food Chains

After the spill, scientists tested plankton that float in the sea. The plankton contained compounds from the oil. Plankton forms the foundation of the food chain. Small fish feed on them. Larger animals feed on the small fish. No one knows how the chemicals will affect the plankton or the animals that eat them. More and more dolphins are showing up on the Gulf Coast. Many are thin and sickly. Scientists believe this may also be linked to the oil spill.

Dangers of Capping

Engineers feared that if they capped the Macondo well, pressure could build up inside the well. The pressure might crack the rocks on the seafloor. This could release most of the 110 million-barrel reservoir of oil beneath the rock. This undersea blowout would have been almost impossible to stop.

Damage to the Deep

Scientists are still studying the spill's long-term effects. They have discovered up to a four-inch (10-cm) thick layer of oil and dead animals on the seafloor. Many sea cucumbers, brittle stars, and other creatures of the deep have died. Coral communities near the Macondo well are dead or dying. But the effects of the spill could have been much worse. The flow of the Mississippi River kept most of the oil offshore. Some of the oil was eaten by oil-eating bacteria, which thrive in the Gulf of Mexico.

Cost of the Spill

On November 15, 2012, two and a half years after the spill, BP plead guilty to criminal charges for its handling of the Gulf oil spill. The company agreed to pay

Oil-Eating Bacteria

At least 16 types of bacteria that are able to eat oil live in the Gulf of Mexico. These bacteria thrived after the Macondo blowout. The bacteria also live in sandy beaches along the Gulf Coast. These organisms helped clean up the oil from the Gulf of Mexico and its beaches.

In this January 2011 photograph, volunteers lay bags filled with oyster shells on shore to restore oyster reefs.

$4 billion in fines. Most of these fines will pay for Gulf restoration projects. In one project, workers are lying down artificial reefs. These reefs will restore habitat for oysters. Oysters are a keystone species. Their reefs protect the shoreline from waves. The reefs also provide food and habitat for birds, crabs, and fish.

EXPLORE ONLINE

Chapter Six focuses on the long-term effects of the oil spill and what people are doing to help the environment. The Web site below focuses on the renewal of the Gulf environment. How is the information on the Web site different from the information in this chapter? What information is the same? How do the two sources present information differently? What can you learn from this Web site?

Renewing the Gulf
www.mycorelibrary.com/gulf-oil-spill

Hardworking Waters

The Gulf of Mexico is one of the hardest working bodies of water in the world. It has been used for fishing, shipping, and drilling oil for years. The Gulf oil spill greatly affected the Gulf Coast's residents, economy, and especially the land and sea wildlife that inhabit it. Due to the attention and money being given to the cause, people are hopeful the region will thrive again. Someday life may flourish in the Gulf once again.

IMPORTANT DATES

2009

BP begins drilling the Macondo well with the Marianas rig in October.

2009

Hurricane Ida hits on November 9 and damages the Marianas rig.

Jan. 31

The Deepwater Horizon oil rig takes over drilling the Macondo oil well.

2010

May 7

BP attempts to lower a containment dome over the leak.

May 19

Oil begins washing up on the Gulf shore.

May 26

BP tries to stop the leak with a top kill and junk shot but fails again.

2010

Apr. 20

The Deepwater Horizon oil rig blowout kills 11 men.

Apr. 22

The Deepwater Horizon oil rig explodes and sinks.

Apr. 25

BP robots try to activate the BOP and fail.

July 12

BP begins work on the capping stack, which eventually stops the leak.

July 15

The US Coast Guard declares the Macondo well dead and the leak stopped.

2012

On November 15, BP pleads guilty to criminal charges and agrees to pay $4 billion in fines.

STOP AND THINK

Why Do I Care?

This book mentions the large amounts of oil the United States uses. How do you and your family use oil? Does oil heat your home? Does it fuel your car? Is oil used to make products that you buy? Write down three ways you can use less oil.

Surprise Me

After reading this book, what two or three facts about the Gulf oil spill surprised you the most? Write a few sentences about each fact. Why did you find them surprising?

You Are There

This book discusses what people did to help after the oil spill. Imagine you live on the Gulf Coast. The oil is coming ashore in your town. How do you react? What do you do? What types of businesses are most affected by the oil spill?

Tell the Tale

Chapter Two talks about the Macondo well blowout. Write 200 words that tell the true story of what happened when the well blew. Describe the sights and the sounds of the blowout. Make sure to set the scene, develop a sequence of events, and write a conclusion.

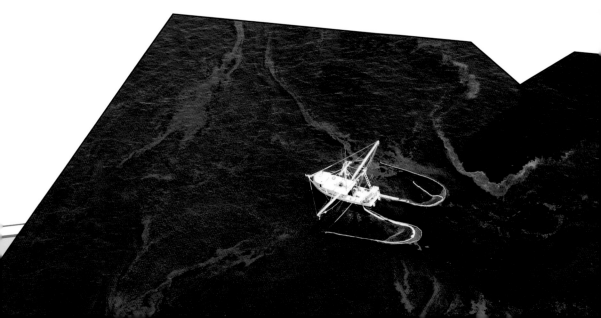

GLOSSARY

blowout preventer (BOP)
a tool made to shut down a well in case of a blowout

capping stack
a heavy piece of equipment used to cap and stop the flow of oil and gas

containment booms
long, plastic-coated fabric tubes made to float on the water and temporarily hold oil in place

containment dome
a dome made to go over leaks and collect oil and gas

drilling mud
a heavy fluid used to grease and cool the drill bit and balance pressure in a well

junk shot
an attempt to block a leak with junk, such as rubber tires and golf balls

keystone species
a species that is central to the survival of many other species in its habitat

mangrove
a tree or bush that grows along tropical coasts

plankton
tiny animals and plants that float in the sea

rookery
a place where nesting birds gather

top kill
an attempt to block a leak with drilling mud

LEARN MORE

Books

Farrell, Courtney. *The Gulf of Mexico Oil Spill.* Edina, MN: ABDO, 2011.

Landau, Elaine. *Oil Spill!: Disaster in the Gulf of Mexico.* Minneapolis: Millbrook Press, 2011.

Peppas, Lynn. *Gulf Oil Spill.* New York: Crabtree, 2011.

Web Links

To learn more about the Gulf oil spill, visit ABDO Publishing Company online at **www.abdopublishing.com**. Web sites about the Gulf oil spill are featured on our Book Links page. These links are routinely monitored and updated to provide the most current information available.

Visit **www.mycorelibrary.com** for free additional tools for teachers and students.

INDEX

ABOUT THE AUTHOR

Linda Crotta Brennan has a master's degree in early childhood education. She taught elementary school and worked in a library. Now she is a full-time writer. She enjoys learning new things and writing about them.